HELP LORD, I MARRIED A GOLFER

Surviving bogeys, sand traps, rain delays, and penalties

Stephanie M. Captain

authorHOUSE®

AuthorHouse™
1663 Liberty Drive
Bloomington, IN 47403
www.authorhouse.com
Phone: 1-800-839-8640

© 2010 Stephanie M. Captain. All rights reserved.

*No part of this book may be reproduced, stored in
a retrieval system, or transmitted by any means
without the written permission of the author.*

First published by AuthorHouse 11/23/2010

ISBN: 978-1-4490-8171-3 (sc)

Printed in the United States of America

This book is printed on acid-free paper.

Certain stock imagery © Thinkstock.

*Because of the dynamic nature of the Internet, any Web addresses or
links contained in this book may have changed since publication and
may no longer be valid. The views expressed in this work are solely those
of the author and do not necessarily reflect the views of the publisher,
and the publisher hereby disclaims any responsibility for them.*

Dedication

To my heavenly Father
for His many blessings.
To my darling husband Amos,
25 years and counting
This book is for you---a great man
I love you very much.
To our legacy—
Amos, Ashley, Aaron
and prince Simien
I adore you.
Mom, I count it a privilege
to be called your daughter,
I love you.
Pastors Pamela & Winston Gardner
I know without a doubt God
brought you into our lives and I am so grateful.
Lastly,
To people everywhere just trying to make it.

CONTENTS

Foreword ... ix

LESSON 1 ... 1
Don't Hinder the Game

LESSON 2 ... 9
If you can't beat them, join them

LESSON 3 ... 17
Don't Impede Progress

LESSON 4 ... 23
There is a method to this madness "Peace and goodwill to all men and peace on ~~earth~~ the home front"

LESSON 5 ... 29
When in Rome do as the Romans

LESSON 6 ... 35
Living Terminology

LESSON 7 ... 41
You do not take the spoil without someone going to war first

LESSON 8 ... 49
Mastery takes time, time, time and more time

Foreword

By Myra D. Sherman

My sister was coming. The last time I saw her she was voicing her opinion as usual. It wasn't that it was wrong, but exactly the opposite, she was always right. She had a vision and no one was going to stop her from reaching her goal. It was simple, she wanted to have a college education, obtain a nice career and ensure that our mother was financially secure. She would never marry anyone that she would have to "one day kill!" She had witnessed the sadness that surrounded our mother's life and she did not want any part of married life. She had recently graduated from high school and wanted to take a vacation prior to spreading her wings, so she came to visit her eldest sister out in the wonderful majestic land of Junction City, Kansas.

This was not my dream but being married to a military man this is where his first tour of duty landed our family. Gone were the days of cowboys carrying six shooters wearing spurs, although on the outskirts of town one could view tumble weeds blowing on the prairie. This city was now filled with military men, women and their families as Fort Riley, Kansas was right around the corner. Junction City was where families awaiting military housing, retired military, past military persons and their families crashed temporarily and sometimes permanently.

My life was monotonous. I went to work at the local golf course and frequented church at least three times weekly. It was not that church was boring, church was refreshing. My life, however, was surrounded by my two boys, a husband, work and church. I was just not up to date on what the local teenagers did to pass the time. As a matter of fact, the only teenagers that I saw were at church service and because there were over seven hundred members, the teenagers and children had their own service in a different part of the sanctuary. This was not going to be easy, keeping my sister entertained, or so I thought.

One day while cashing out a costumer, Amos walked in with his usual buddies and pleasingly pleasant personality and it hit me. He was young, single and seemingly nice; would he be interested in taking my sister out for the three weeks that she was visiting? He was interested, so I promised him I would bring her picture to work the next day. That night my husband warned me not to meddle in matters that concerned the heart, but my mind was made up. I rummaged through pictures of my family and found the picture from her Debutant Cotillion. She looked like a princess. Her gown was elegant and tended to accentuate every curve that she had. The makeup and the hairstyle were so befitting that the complete package would make Cinderella hand Prince Charming right over to my sister.

Apparently Amos thought so too. When I showed him the picture it was as though golfing was not the first love of his life any more. It was as if the world stopped rotating and he was losing all sense of life as it was a few moments prior. As I reflect back it seemed as though Amos was literally salivating as he looked at that picture.

They met and the rest is history. My sister's thoughts of education and career changed. Ten weeks after their introduction, they stood in my living room and exchanged marriage vows. Three children, a grandchild and twenty-five years later I still see the same look in his eyes as he stares at her when she is not looking. This is usually when he is headed out the door with his golf bag in tow.

LESSON 1

Don't Hinder the Game

Years ago when I first married my husband I could not comprehend anyone loving a sport as much as he did golf. Being the teenager that I was, one day I decided to check up on his putting skills. I had to make sure his clubs were the only thing he was playing with. At the time we lived in Germany (my first time away from home and living in the German community) and he worked less than one mile from the golf course. Exactly. Enough said. Most days when my husband's work day ended guess where he went? You know it, the golf course. Now at that time we only had one car. I did not even have a driver's license, so to get around I would have to take the city bus several miles to the installation. Then I had to walk from the bus stop and on up the hill to the golf course to see if I could find my runaway husband. Germany is beautiful Country. It is no stranger to the natural beauty found in good old fashion nature. So forcing my way through the rough and tree branches I would do a massive search from hole to hole trying to see what I could see. I couldn't take the route the golfers took of course. I stayed on the little trails praying I did not run into any wildlife. From hole to hole and tree to tree I used my investigative skills until finally, bam! There he was. Guess who was in his company? A nine iron, a golf tee, a putter and a towel and they were having the time of their lives. I could not allow my scenic trip to be in vain so I stood there for a while unobserved and watched him play. I soon discovered he was pretty darn good at what he did. Ok, so I had made a complete fool of myself, now what?

When you know this (the game or whatever it is) is what your man loves, then you should do all you can to help him get there. If he is playing with his golf balls duh… he IS playing with his golf balls. Knowing there is no competition between golf and you must be your reality. Irons, sand wedges, pitching wedges, and drivers can also work FOR you if you know how to use them. It is more than wisdom to set aside and agree upon times that he will be able to simply enjoy playing the game.

I cannot tell you how long my husband has been playing golf on Saturday mornings. It is a double digit number that I have grown to love. I sleep in during those times and spend time with the children that I missed during the week while working my 9-5 and shuffling them back and forth to daycare. In later years I developed other methods to enjoying myself while he chased the little white ball around, but that is a lesson I will get to later in the book.

It is amazing how we as people can sometimes concentrate on the negative. Anything worth having, anything that will be successful will take time, be it, marriage or muse. How can a sand wedge and a driver help you? To my husband golf was his Oasis in certain aspects. We all need one no matter who we are or where we hailed from. Most can benefit from learning to relax a bit more. I often joke about my husband's golf clubs and their many travels. No matter where we go or what type of road trip we take the golf clubs are the first thing in the car ninty-five percent of the time. If we are having space issues or comfort struggles he works it out somehow as to not exempt his sidekicks. Some people know cities by their attractions and tourist sites, my family, including our three children have come to know cities by their golf courses. It's normal for us. The old saying goes, "If mama ain't happy, ain't nobody happy." I beg to differ. If big daddy is satisfied, mama is getting what she wants, and I can live with that. When we are looking for vacation or getaway spots the first thing we look for are accommodations and golf courses. It wasn't always like this though.

It is of the utmost importance to set a good foundation so you can build a healthy relationship. You must set boundaries in your marriage or relationship so that it is established on love, trust and respect. Most people go into a relationship with preconceived notions established by lessons taught or experienced by others. The foundation is already set that will dictate how you will handle, trouble, tests, and temptation; and it will be the deciding factor of the health of your relationships. The lessons you learn before meeting the love of your life should not inhibit, restrict, or inflict your relationships, but enhance them. You may not always be able to judge a situation by how or what another person did or did not do because you are not in a relationship with that individual. You must be able to recognize your spouse's moods, body language, tone's, and temperament to live well together. What another does may or may not work for your relationship, so it is best to get to know one another. What they like, what they need, how they want it and when, will be the eagle of your union.

I met my husband through my sister Myra who knew him from her place of employment, which just happened to be the golf course (as she told in the forward). I was first introduced to him because of the game of golf. It is what he did, who he was before I ever came into the picture. Golf was a huge part of his recreation BEFORE marriage. What can you learn here?

1. **No extras**
   You will have enough to overcome without adding unnecessary challenges to your relationships. Never try to change a person to become what you want them to be. I see people do this with hobbies, pastimes, children from previous relationships, etc. You destroy the foundation if you come into a relationship trying to replace the foundation already set choosing to ignore the significance of what is already in place. If it is of value to him it should be valuable to you.

~ Valuable lesson~

When you come into something new, i.e. job, position, relationships, it is best to sit back and become familiar with the environment before you decide to make changes. Observe for a little while before you start to give advice and make changes.

2. **Do the math**
   It is best to see how you can add to-- not subtract, extract or hinder what means so much to your spouse. You may or may

not want to participate in your spouse's hobbies but it is imperative to find a way to support them. You may have to be their biggest cheerleader, fan club, or motivator, but always be a part of the solution and a part of his pleasure.

3. **Don't hinder the game**
   You can make a sport out of anything. If you begin to see the game as an extension of who you are as a couple it becomes far easier to support. Doing a sports theme for parties or get-togethers and learning more about this "thing" they love can make for some interesting conversations. This will keep you in the fairway; and that is a good thing. I often hear women say, "My man doesn't talk." I assure you he is talking. The question is, "to whom?"

Which brings me to my next lesson.

LESSON 2

If you can't beat them, join them

I learned how to play the game of golf and it actually was a lot of fun and my honey was glad to have me as his pupil. He loved me and this was one more thing we could do together. I wanted to be with him and he with me so I learned to play on his turf; at least in this particular arena. Now let me just say this. No relationship can be one-sided so I don't want you to get the wrong impression. My husband is one of the most giving persons I have ever met. He continually gives to me and his family and it is something I never want to take for granted. One of the things that drew me to him was his crazy sense of humor and his caring ways. There are not too many things I can name that I ask him to do for or with me that he will say no to. This alone made me want to share in what was so special to him, but I just did not know how at first. For one thing I did not know one person that played golf before I met him. Not one soul. I did not watch it on television and I paid no attention to it in the news; until I met Sgt. Captain.

Most people have heard the phrase, "opposites attract", and it was true in my marriage, but it only added to our relationship. If the situation aroused I could converse with him or his friends about the sport of golf. Usually I was the only female on most occasions when it came to the Americans playing the game while living in Europe. We were newlyweds and we were sharing so many firsts; our first apartment together, our first car, first fights, and make-up sessions. So while we were still getting to know each other I tagged along with some of his sports. Golf was ok and I loved to bowl so it worked for us. Life was good until he just stayed too long on the golf course. It wasn't that he went, it was that he stayed entirely too long when he did.

Word to the wise, in any relationship you must have at least one thing as a minimum you can share as a couple that does not include: paying bills, the children, family members, friends, or work. My husband and I love games, all kinds of games and we do a lot of that as well as taking walks, watching movies and just talking.

For some people talking on the phone is recreation. I am not one of those people. I will text, e-mail, and even face-book from time to time, but I judge my relationships with my real friends by how much time we spend together. It doesn't have to be often, but if we are friends and you can never make it to my home, my functions, at some point and time, say never, then we are only acquaintances. It is a good thing for me to know where my relationships stand. This wholes true to any relationship, but especially marriage. You have to know where you stand with each other in relation to what is important. I have heard it said, "Some things go without saying," but no I beg to differ. There are many things that must be said, and you will not make it successful, happy, and peaceful until they are.

1. **First up**
   Couples should clearly define their expectations. You must never guess or assume anything. Unless someone speaks up, needs go unmet, and that means penalties; some that can, if unchecked, be hard to overcome. Communication is the first art of any relationship. I do not agree that the honeymoon phase ever has to end, but reality will make visitations. When it does it will be important to know one another. This will continue throughout your relationship.

2. **Never stand back**
   Be apart, don't wish, hope, or wonder. Step it up and do you in whatever arena you find yourself in. Be confident in who you are and keep the passion that drew you and your spouse together. Do not make the fatal mistake of being consumed with or transforming into what or who your spouse is or what you think they want you to be. Be you and embrace who they are, but do not lose yourself trying to please, manipulate, and control. It will only breed bitterness and anger in later days. The biggest championship you will ever be in is called marriage.

3. **Find the balance**
   Joining in doesn't always mean physical presence. Being there after whatever event,

> game, or cause that you were unable to attend is important as well. The focus here is if you can't be a part, then find a part; a place where you can make the statement loud and clear, "I'm here and I support you no matter where life takes us." That's joining in. Being supportive may be all you need to do, depending on your relationship

Having served 26 years in the military my husband spent many nights away from our home. Sometimes this meant days, weeks, and even months apart from me, and later our children. My husband has this thing about him that just drives him to make the most out of any situation. When he went to the war, he found something he liked to do although he was on the front lines of enemy territory. When he went TDY (temporary duty assignment) after work he played golf. No matter what State or state he found himself in, he did what he loved. Initially I was resentful of this. In my eyes he was away and I was working fulltime and taking care of sick children and just plain worn out and low and behold, he had time to play golf. After a little while I woke up and learned from his principal. Do what you love. Make the most of every situation. I learned how to leave that last bit of laundry and take a walk, even if it meant taking the kids. Read a book if only a couple of pages before going to bed. Write a poem on my lunch break. I realized the world would not end if I did not have a spotless house, perfect children or gourmet meals. Even if I chose not to go to the golf course with him, I joined his methods and became a better person.

You must learn how to deal with the wind because it is guaranteed to blow. This should never be a shock. It is nature, just like the rain and the thunderstorms, as well as extreme heat. My husband's golf bag has an umbrella, a wind breaker, and an extra shirt. This bag also includes extra balls, tees, and various clubs; driver, woods, and irons. All play differently and affect the shot differently, but for him to be prepared he must have them in his bag and know how to use them. When faced with challenging weather he has a choice to keep playing the game or quit. You will always have those same choices in your relationship. The factor here is how important winning is to you. Have a plan. If this happens how will we or more importantly "I" handle it? Ask yourself real questions. What will make me leave? What can't I forgive (meaning not willing to work at the relationship any longer)? Who can come between us? You must give a definition to your fears before you can ever discredit them. Give them a name: infidelity, bankruptcy, in-laws, x-wives, step children, sickness. Life really is not a fairytale, but it is a dream that can include a nightmare or two.

Hence, my next lesson

LESSON 3

Don't Impede Progress

Yes, I learned how to play golf. Yes, I learned the language, and yes I grew to love the peaceful nature of the course itself. I found it very soothing and it helped me in my spirituality. Not to mention it was great exercise. But, I grew bored, very quickly. My husband had a hearty appetite for golf and nine holes was just not enough. Plus, the fact that I used the holes to do my own personal photo shots did not help the matter much. I went from hole to hole posing this way and that, even interchanging my accessories having the time of my life and getting in the way. He would never have said that, but in this life you must be able to be honest with yourself. Golf was his out. He was elated to share it with me but this was his time to relax and let off some steam of a highly stressful job and he deserved that. Golf was in no way a threat to me. If anything it was an asset; plus, the fact that there is no equation that involved me plus the sun all day. It was fun driving the golf cart and walking the course getting a little exercise and tiring the children out. We had a blast at the driving range while he was working on his putt or chipping balls. Other than the occasional recreation trip, I gave up chasing balls and allowed him to develop his skill.

I remember when I was pregnant with our second child. It was a very difficult pregnancy to say the very least. I was high risk and in and out of the hospital all the time. When I finally got to 36 weeks I was taken off bed rest and what a feeling that was to get out of the house and "do" something. Needless to say, we went to the golf course. My husband, our son, and my sister and I all got in the car and went for some family fun. My husband pretended to play a serious game of golf while we followed him from hole to hole in the golf cart. I was far too pregnant to drive the cart so my sister was glad to pitch in and help out (she is that kind of person). By the end of the day we had almost overturned the cart, nearly flipped it over the bridge, and backed it over my poor husband. We look back on these "outings" and laugh now. The truth of the matter is when it is time for the real game, preparation for tournaments or scrambles he needs to give it his all and he can't do that chasing me. That comes later.

1. **"Out"**
   Whatever the out for you and your mate, it must be emphasized as deserving and both rewarding. Every person must have one. Golf is my spouse's time to let off steam and relax and everyone deserves that right; within reason of course. Keep this in mind. If there is no "tee" or "me" time it can take a toll on the relationship. He plays golf and other sports and I do my thing and when we come together again there are no rain delays but clear skies.

2. **Dictations and Limitations**
   It is imperative to set times and limitations to include outings that include each other. That means you must communicate when each other has plans or needs plans to do or go, if not conflict is inevitable. My husband knows except for a big tournament, no golf on Sunday. In the same token, I understand that there must be practice days in preparation to certain events. But this is all communicated, most of the time.

3. **Organic anyone**
   Relationships are living breathing representations of who we are, where we have been and where we plan to go. They must be fed and nourished continually if they are to grow and remain healthy. You should give them your best without the residue of past relationships. If you find yourself deficient in an area do what it takes to make your relationship vital, alive, and joyful.

LESSON 4

There is a method to this madness
"Peace and goodwill to all men and
peace on ~~earth~~ the home front"

ESSAYS

It was not long before I begin to view the game of golf not solely as competition, but those 18 holes soon became therapeutic. My hubby is one of the most fun loving energetic people you could ever meet, it's just his personality. You don't have to take my word for it just ask anyone that he comes in contact with and they will tell you the same thing. In time I began to notice that our time together; our conversations, our play, or just being together was so much better after he finished his game. Almost like coming back from a well deserved vacation. There was a new outlook, a better perspective, a warm atmosphere. This held true no matter how his day was before those 18 holes, it just all seemed to dissipate for both of us. People often say, "You can catch more flies with honey," and boy is that a true statement. When I ranted and raved about my hubby being gone all the time, no matter how right I was, I did not get the results I intended. The truth of the matter is; he knew what he was doing so my telling him in the manner I did only strained our relationship. You must learn the skill of repackaging. Deliver the same message; just wrap it in a beautiful container. Most times it is not what you say, but how and when you choose to say it.

1. **Cheers**
   We (I had to be the initiator) made it a point to make the most of our time when he returned from his games, tournaments, deployments, field assignments, TDY, what have you. He was gone a lot already so we figured, why waste time fighting when you already have so little time together? If more people thought this way it would make a world of difference. Enjoy your time together and celebrate each other whenever.

2. **Flying objects**
   I heard an adolescent who was making a guest appearance on a popular game show say he had a fear of objects flying around his head and I thought, that was interesting. The young man, about 12 years old proceeded to say that he and his father were in an open field hitting golf balls back and forth to one another and his father forget to say "fore" and he was stroke in the head with the golf ball. OK, that had to hurt I thought, but as the show continued the host, who shall remain nameless, responded that you must pay attention when you have objects in the air. Now if he knew his dad had hit the ball, duh…it is coming back. At least pay attention and look up at the very least. Like they say in the church, "Arm yourselves accordingly." Look up anything

you can to arm yourself with resources or counsel, to help your relationship. Good advice that is. Just know that everyone is not qualified to give this type of advice.

3. **No Trespassing**

   If it is one thing my husband knows about me, it is I do not have anything to do with anything that has more legs than I do. That being said, I make it a point not to create an atmosphere that is inviting to critters and rodents. I on purpose create an atmosphere that is uninviting to such creatures. In addition to this, I keep a good exterminator because country living can sometimes bring surprises. The same holds true to the people I allow in my home, my relationships, and my life in general. This includes who is allowed to give me advice. Everyone just is not qualified. Rodents carry germs, poison, disease, and are just all around creepy, and so are some people. Why would I want poison in my home? It would not make sense to have something so potentially harmful to me in my intimate space, not to mention exposing it to my family. That being said, what about relationships that can affect and effect you and your marriage in the same way? I do not believe in having male bashing, peace crashing, or momentary cashers (people that pry on you for their gain then leave once they have what they want) in my life.

LESSON 5

When in Rome do as the Romans

My husband was busy cultivating his craft. I should be doing the same thing? Or at the very least, shopping; no just kidding, well not entirely, some shopping is warranted. Everyone has something they like to do, have a passion for, would love to do or constantly dream of doing. I have heard it referred to as a gift, a craft, a passion, and even a destiny, but no one is exempt from that "thing" that makes you drive past opposition, pressure and mocking. For some it may be one thing and others may have many things. For my husband one of his things is mastering the game of golf. No doubt, he is committed to doing whatever it takes to accomplish his goal. I know without a doubt he is going to chase that little white ball because it gives him a certain satisfaction. Since the day I met my husband golf has been a part of our lives so I know it is an important part. It was a while before this revelation came to fruition for me. When it finally hit home, the principal, the persistence, and the prerequisite of the sport, I realized I played as well. Only my playing ground was mastering at life, not eighteen holes. You must be diligent and dedicated to who you are and what you believe. This I learned from my golfer and my God.

When our oldest son was a toddler he loved to go outside. He could barely walk but he wasn't afraid to explore his surroundings. One beautiful afternoon I decided to let him walk ahead of me and soon his little waddle became a run. He giggled having the time of his life until suddenly he began to scream. He would walk to the left, then right, pace, then scream some more. Concerned and confused about his actions I carefully assessed the situation only to discover that the source of his unrest was his shadow. Based on his level of fear, he thought it was the bogy man no doubt, but it was only his own shadow. What was making him so uncomfortable was a part of him that he had not become familiar with. It was the part of him that presented itself only as a result of certain circumstances.

1. **Mirrors**
   What you see is not always what you get. What you see in a mirror is a image of what is being reflected. What you need to see and know about yourself comes from within. Hints of who you really are shows up on the outside. Knowing your strengths, weaknesses, likes, dislikes, wants, and needs and being able to communicate them honestly will eliminate much discord. You must know: who you are in a crisis, who you are in boredom, who you are in idleness, and who you are in opposition. This is the only true picture you will have of self. Know you, before you enter any relationship.

2. **Championships**

   Even when you are on a team everyone gets the same trophy, rewards, and perks, because it is a team effort. This does not eliminate the opportunities for personal rewards and prizes. You can still be closest to the pin, have the longest drive, hole in one; with respect to golf, when it comes to competition. Who you are is not solely dependent on the team. No one and nothing can complete you, that is a God job. Do not give your spouse, lover, or friends, the responsibility of completing you. It is far too big a job for any person. When you know who you are in yourself and in your relationships, it releases others from having to figure it out; therefore, eliminating frustrations.

3. **Sand bags**

   Each year we see the devastation of hurricanes in our country. Many times the aftermath does more damage than the storms themselves. Growing up on the east coast I've seen much preparation for inclement weather. It is not unusual to see sand bags being used to help offset some of the damage that can be done. It would be silly to do such preparations when there is no storm. Learn not to create crisis. Surrounding your home with sandbags when there is no storm is extra. Going into your relationship without knowing who you are and what you want out of life is like wearing handcuffs and blindfolds. You have no vision and no direction, and that is baggage.

LESSON 6

Living Terminology

A bogey is one stroke more than is required to complete a successful play on a hole. Most golfers would not be very happy if they bogie each hole. To par is far better and eagles and birdies are exceptional. It makes the game exciting and that is where competition begins. Marriages are no different. It is all about the score. Par is average. Most people are fine with mediocrity, but a true competitor can never accept average. When a score card reads eagle or birdie or even on the rare occasion, hole in one, things happen. I soon discovered that I could control where the 19th hole would be. You will not always be in the fairway but you can control what and how you get the ball back on course.

What can I learn from golf? You cannot live off "hole in ones." Relationships are built on everyday ordinary moments not solely on special events. Special events are wonderful reminders of where you have been and where you are headed, but they can never be the focal point of a relationship. What happens when you can't go, buy, or do? There are still two people that must establish who they are not based on things or events.

1. **Learn how to read a score card**
   Know how to rate yourself so you can deal with the outcome of the game. You must really be honest and give yourself the proper score. There is no way for you to improve your "game" or relationship if it is built on lying and cheating. When you cease to be honest with yourself because you want to appear to be okay to people who are judging from the outside, you are in a dangerous place. It is fine to need improvement, that's life. But needing people's approval at the expense of the person you live with is called betrayal, which can equate to trouble.

2. **Take the drop**
   Move forward from where you are when at all possible. The greatest gift you can ever give a person besides love is forgiveness. Let the past be the past. When it comes to disagreements, I have learned a bit of wisdom. There will be no playing on the back nine, i.e. sleeping on the sofa, locking the bedroom door, or shutting down. I may get upset enough to not turn off the lights and light a candle but, that just means we will be leaving the light on that night. It is more fun anyway. You can't always be in control of when it is time to talk, but it is wisdom to be there until. This doesn't mean pretending the problem isn't there. Nor does it mean not being able to express

your feelings. It simply means you will not allow that "thing" to come between the two of you. It should never be you the problem and him, but you and him, then the problem.

LESSON 7

You do not take the spoil without someone going to war first

When we lived on Fort Polk in Louisiana my husband was the Post champion of the golf course. Oh what a proud moment for us as a family, but more so for him after spending so much time trying to improve his game. There was an article in the newspaper about this event which leads to him doing a series of follow up articles with him giving tips on mastering particular holes of that same golf course. This win had some fringed benefits other than adding to the collection of trophies he was starting to build. This was the first time he had been given his own parking space. One day I drove up to the course and there the sign stood reading, "Post Champion" and underneath was my husband's name. It did not take me long at all to realize I was his Mrs., and I drove my car right into that parking space. If anyone knows anything about military life, then they would understand that parking is a biggie on any installation because there never seems to be enough. I did not play one round of golf in that tournament, but I still enjoyed the benefit of his hard work, determination, and skill. He was the only one that faced the heat. He was the one that prepared himself mentally and physically to win. Not to mention facing the elements; the heat in Louisiana can be vicious to say the very least.

At some point you must transition and see your companion's sport, hobby, or pastime, as a profession. Even if it is to professionally bring him joy and pleasure, this is a benefit worth pursuing. He may not rule the world, but he should be the hero in your home. It is vital to never lose that love, that passion and joy from the early stages of your relationship. I still get excited when it is time for my husband to come home. I look forward to date nights, our walks, and just hanging out. Recreate the magic as often as possible. It is not always easy and it will take work. When you know what you have is not being valued; speak up or plan something so that your good times are not a thing of the past.

1. **No PGA today!**
   People **G**etting **A**ttitudes

   Every stage, phase, and age has an emotional attachment to it. Deal with it and keep it moving. If you have a bad day, remember the people you love are the good part in that day. They should not feel the brunt of the chaos. Attitude usually has a negative stigma to it. What it really equates to is this, an emotional display of disappointment. Don't let disappointment drive you to destruction. Remember it can take much more time to rebuild than it does for good maintenance or renovation.

2. **Chipping and putting**
It is a well known fact that no matter how long you can drive the ball, if you are unable to chip or putt you don't have a good game. Yes, you must be able to go the distance in your relationship, but not to the extent of becoming bitter, resentful or existence. Manage those small things that chip or eat away at your relationship because they have a great impact on the outcome of your relationship. A termite is very small, but it will destroy a home if left unchecked. It amazes me when I talk to people and the reason they are having trouble is because of something that happen years ago, but they are still carrying it around today. Stop reliving the past. You only revisit the past for the purpose of healing or helping others, otherwise, get a current address.

3. **Repairing divots**
Some things may impact your relationships to the point of damage. Make repairs, do the maintenance. In the game of golf it is mandatory to repair divots or damage done to putting greens made by **your** ball. If you do not do this very important task, it can impact your game. If the mark is not fixed within a certain time frame the grass will die, costing the golf course money and impacting the other members of the club. Figure out what is best for you and yours and execute your plans

when things happen that require fixing. Don't wait. An old house can sometimes require new paint, repairs, or remodeling, but the fact of the matter is, a new house and an older house give the same thing; shelter. Value what you have. Make a big deal about who you have---celebrate, live, enjoy and give it your all so that whatever the future brings you have no regrets. The grass is never greener on the other side because it is left idle. All grass must be cared for. You must cut it, treat it, trim it, kill weeds from it, water it, and plant new seeds. Maintenance is a must. This should not be viewed as a chore. The excitement should be knowing the hard work will pay off. You know the end result, all things being equal, should be satisfaction.

I went to a Lenten retreat a few years ago with a very close friend. This was a totally new experience for me, but I really needed some quiet time in my life. The entire stay we could not have or use cell phones or computers. There was one phone designated for emergency calls only. Our room had two small beds and a nightstand. No television or radio. The place was designed to shut out the frustrations of the world and regain your inner peace. We ate each meal together as a group. When the bell rang we all gathered together for prayer. This took place several times during the day. The monastery had a beautiful garden that was meant to be enjoyed by its guest. I love flowers and this garden to me was a flower haven. The smell, the color, the serenity of it all was just like giving my soul a bath. There were many places to find solace there and I took my escape as often as possible. Being the people watcher I can sometimes be, I noticed something very peculiar one afternoon. Walking through the garden was a lady with a sign attached to her that read, "Silent Retreat." Needless to say I was quite curious. All of us were on a retreat, but why or how could one's be silent? When I enquired of my friend later, she brought some clarity to my observation. The monastery was their place to find the quiet they needed without the interference of unwanted conversation and useless activity. Rather than trying to explain that to everyone, these signs served as their billboards. Everyone needs a place they can go with no distractions, discord, or drama. You must have a place designated as a no attitude zone. For my spouse and I it is our bedroom. There we make love, not war. We talk about our dreams and cares, make plans, but we never want it to be a place where either of us dread going. We may go to the park, on a walk, drive or sit in the back yard to talk seriously, but we try our best to keep it outside because home should and must always be a refuge. You may not be able to always getaway, but you have to put away those things that suck the life out of your relationship to reconnect with what is good. What is worth keeping? What is worth fighting for?

LESSON 8

Mastery takes time, time, time and more time

Sand traps are specifically designed to create a problem, therefore, should be avoided. Should you have the misfortune of getting your ball into one, depending on the level of your skills, it could be time consuming and costly; to your game. At best it could cost you a stroke or two and that alone could cost you your competition, unless, you know how to handle sand. Even after getting out of the sand, the trap itself still requires maintenance. You are required to take a rake and clean up the mess you have made so that should someone else come along and fall into the same trap your mistakes do not influence the outcome of their game.

Most people I know, especially woman, do not care to walk around with sand in their shoes. Walking the beach is one thing, but day to day living with this sand would become quite annoying. It doesn't feel right and it can cause skin irritation because the shoe is not the purpose for which it was intended. Nagging has the same affect. It tends to rub people the wrong way.

1. **You are going to have to accept the routine**
   Put on your SAG (Support a Golfer) belt
   and hold on tight because the ride can get

bumpy without it. If you don't strap it on damage is inevitable. This will hold you down when questions, reasoning's, and disloyalty rears its ugly head. This belt represents the trust and truth factors in a marriage and is directly linked to courage and confidence. The truth will come out about how you really feel about "the game" when the routine greets you like the morning sun. If you are a BAG (bitter about golf) or anything in your relationship it will show up with a vengeance. Everybody needs and wants support. If you are truly devoted it will show and eventually it will pay some good dividends.

2. **Don't get caught in the time trap**
    You must without a doubt learn how to tell GOLF time. **G**et **O**ver **L**eaving **F**ast-----it is not in the wives hand book, but I promise you it will help your relationship immensely. I have almost become an expert at telling golf time. When my husband says, "I have two more holes", I know that means I can go and run an errand or even take a nap and will be finished about the same time. When he tells me he has nine more holes, I can go and spend some well deserved time looking at estate sales and window shopping. When he says he is playing in a tournament, well, I have learned to plan for us to have dinner together and have a little evening fun. Things always

work well in a relationship when there is proper communication. Notice I said that I learned to tell golf time. It wasn't something he explained or could explain he had been programmed when I stepped into a world of greens. Until I figured out this mystical time I spent many hours waiting because I had the wrong numeric system. What is not written in the golf rules is the time that is takes to brag about the game after the game is played. Nor does anyone mention the extra holes just for the sake of the game.

3. **Appreciate the craft**
   A little respect goes a long way. I don't say a lot sometimes because I learn much from observation. When my husband is getting ready for a big tournament he goes through a whole regime. Other than this he does routine maintenance on his clubs and other golf equipment.

Know that you too can benefit from the use of a good set of golf clubs. I remember when my husband and I first returned from living overseas. We rented our first state-side apartment and begin to settle in nicely. This was very short lived. During this time he always went to field exercises, training, and anything else the Army deemed necessary. This meant my baby and I were at home alone most of the time. To my horror, one night while I was out, our apartment was burglarized. My neighbor had spotted the lookout guy and thwarted the robbery, but not before they packed up our things and went through all of our stuff. I was devastated. It is just something unnerving and violating about someone going through your home.

That night we had to sleep in the living room floor right next to the door. The window that the robbers broke could not be repaired until morning. I was just a wreck and refused to close my eyes for fear of someone coming back in that window again. It was two in the morning. My husband, still in field uniform, lay next to me beside the door. My baby lay on my chest and in my right hand was a golf club, an iron to be exact. Suddenly I heard a crash. Delirious from sleep deprivation and being traumatized, I sat straight up and begin screaming to the top of my lungs. My dear sweet husband being the protector he is, jumped up, opened the door, and ran out into the night leaving me in hysterias. Obviously, he had a strategy that he neglected to share with me. He and the neighbor, armed and dangerous, thought it best to deal with the would be robbers outside. All I could think of is that they are back, but I do have a club and I am not afraid to use it. My husband and his sidekick did a thorough search of the premises, but could not find the intruders. Returning to the inside of the apartment they did another search only to find no one. Mystified, and certain of what I heard (breaking glass), I joined in the search. I am not sure if it was instinct or formula that lead me to the kitchen. There I found the intruder. Lying in the sink amidst the dishes left to dry was the culprit; a frozen chicken. Apparently, it had fallen over into the sink, gravity being its accomplice. That night had been such a nightmare I forgot I had been planning to make sweet and sour chicken for the church pot luck the next day.

My husband uses his golf clubs one way and I use them another. They benefit me just as much as they benefit him. When my husband and I go walking through our neighborhood it is the golf club we take to ward off possible creatures. I use them for objects out of my reach. The night of the break in I used them as a weapon. The kids have a set, and now even our one year old grandson waddles through the house with a club in each hand. Make life work for you. It can be a beautiful journey.

The Code

1. Never, never, ever tell him to, "Take his clubs and shove them" (at least not where he can hear you).

2. Hit not thy husband with an iron!

3. No aiding and abetting golf equipment (this includes backing over it with the car).

4. Sell not thou husband's golf clubs in a garage sale.

5. Thou shall not put his golf tees in the fire place.

6. Thou shall not become a heckler.

7. The score card is the little black book you don't throw away.

8. Golf carts are driven over bridges, not into them.

9. Trophies are not paperweights.

10. You do NOT get parking privileges for his handicap.

A note from the Author

I am not a Counselor

I am not an Advisor

I am a woman who has been married to the love of her life for 25years. The information in this book is based on my experience as the wife of a golfer. Everyone's experience is unique. I just thought I would share mine and in some small way let my wonderful husband know how much I appreciate the wonderful husband he is. I give information and I pray that this information is useful to you in some way. If it made you laugh or think, then to God be the glory.

Stephanie

Contact Information
Stephanie M. Captain
P. O. Box 7713
Augusta, GA 30905
speakforme@hotmail.com

NOTES

NOTES

NOTES

NOTES

NOTES

NOTES